Revenge is the Best Exercise

ALSO BY DAVID BRENNER

Soft Pretzels with Mustard

DAVID BRENNER

Revenge is the Best Exercise

Illustrations by Nick Siracuse
Photographs by Mark Chin

ARBOR HOUSE
New York

Copyright © 1984 by David Brenner

All rights reserved, including the right of reproduction in whole or in part in any form. Published in the United States of America by Arbor House Publishing Company and in Canada by Fitzhenry & Whiteside, Ltd.

Library of Congress Cataloging in Publication Data

Brenner, David, 1945-
   Revenge is the best exercise.

   1. Exercise—Anecdotes, facetiae, satire, etc.
I. Title.
PN6231.E9B74   1984   818'.5407   84-16869
ISBN 0-87795-655-3 (alk. paper)

Manufactured in the United States of America

10 9 8 7 6 5 4 3 2 1

This book is printed on acid free paper. The paper in this book meets the guidelines for permanence and durability of the Committee on Production Guidelines for Book Longevity of the Council on Library Resources.

Design by Stanley S. Drate/Folio Graphics Co., Inc.

*To my two-year-old son,
Cole Jay,
who stands only two feet, eleven inches,
but makes me feel ten feet tall*

CONTENTS

ACKNOWLEDGMENTS	11
INTRODUCTION	13
WAKING UP	15
THE BATHROOM	18
GETTING DRESSED	24
MEALS AT HOME	29
HOUSEWORK	31
SHOPPING	36
DRIVING TO WORK	37
ELEVATORS AND ESCALATORS	43
THE OFFICE	44
CONVERSATION	55
DINING OUT	62
ETHNIC EXERCISES	68
DANCING	71
SEX	73
HOLIDAYS	76
MAKE BELIEVE	99
WHEN YOU DO THIS	102
THINKING TO BURN UP FAT	105
MISCELLANEOUS HELPFUL HINTS	107
CALORIE-BURNING ACTIVITIES	116
SPORTS	120
CONCLUSION	125

ACKNOWLEDGMENTS

My thanks to Arbor House for believing in another one of my ideas; Steve Reidman, my personal manager, who encouraged me to stay up all night writing while he slept; Artie Moskowitz, my William Morris agent, who never wasted my writing time by putting me on hold; George Schultz, owner of Pips in Sheepshead Bay, for his zany comments and suggestions; Dr. Milton Reder, my physician, for keeping my chronic back pain dormant so I could have the physical strength and stamina to sit and type; my sister, Bib, for her clever ideas and total undying support; my secretary, Susan A. Bennett, for her endless typing; and my fans, who throughout my career have always backed my crazy ideas, including this one, I hope.

Special thanks to Nick Siracuse for his wonderful stick drawings and his ideas, and to my brother and creative consultant, Mel Brenner, for his superb guidance and excellent contribution of additional material.

And a very, very special thanks to my mother and father because their love has made all things in my life possible.

P.S. None of the above persons exercise.

INTRODUCTION

What am I doing writing an exercise book? Is it to join the great American craze for exercising and staying in good physical shape? No! It is just the opposite. I have written this book for those of us who either don't have what it takes to become a jogger, weight lifter, aerobic, an aquaobic, star gymnast, karate or kung fu expert, or *do* have what it takes, *but* would like to achieve the same physical results without the time and strain. This book is also for all of us who get sick to our stomachs watching people dress up in exercise uniforms of matching color and texture and then take to the streets. It is for those who share my disgust for stores that specialize in wristbands, headbands, anklebands, kneebands, waistbands, music to go with your dancing, jumping, bending, turning, twisting, folding, ripping, leaping, crushing, matting, and flipping.

Running to lose fat that never seems to come off, toning muscles that refuse to tone, fantasizing about becoming the popular person one can never become—I am tired of the physical fitness fad. It has gotten out of hand. Everyone in America is training for an Olympic event in which he or she, in a million years, will never be able to participate. What is going on? Why have we become so physically oriented and how have we gotten so sucked into this multibillion-dollar industry?

This is your chance to get into better shape, which is something we all should do, but without the malarkey. I'm in pretty good shape. I don't belong to a gymnasium; I don't have equipment all over my apartment; I don't join people jogging in the street. I have my own way of doing it, which I find to be an inexpensive way of preparing myself for plain old better health and fitness. There is no strain. There is no sweat. There are no aches. There are no pains. As a matter of fact, I think it is a lot of fun. The only expense you are going to have is the one you have already absorbed—the purchase of this book. You read this. You do what is written here and you will be as fit as any other human being, and no one will even notice that you are exercising, not even you. Here is an everyman's and everywoman's everyday approach to everyday activities. Everything you do in life can be turned into a painless, fun exercise. You don't have to buy anything special and you don't have to wear anything special. All you have to do is be yourself, with a couple of minor alterations. I hope that this will change your life for the better.

And now, my fellow protesters, join me in becoming physically fit, without pain, without expense, without sweat.

Waking Up

It is possible to exercise, from the time you first open your eyes until you close them to go to sleep, without even straining yourself. All you have to do is make minor adjustments to the everyday, mundane, and hardly ever noticed activities. A little switch here, a little switch there; an extra bend and an extra pull; an extra reach and an extra little something that will tone your muscles and help wear away that excessive body tissue.

Let us begin at the beginning: you wake up. Oh, sure, I know what you're thinking, right away you're going to have to put on a special outfit and roll around on the floor, lifting and pulling and straining and sweating, running and moaning, and hurting and groaning. No way. I'm talking about the everyday human activity known simply as waking up. Wake up a new way. Wake up doing something for your physical well-being.

Here is a simple procedure to follow from that moment when you first come alive, all the way through your day until you close your eyes and go to sleep at night. You will be exercising without even knowing it. Okay, now it's time to get in shape. Time to wake up!

When your alarm sounds don't drowsily reach over to turn it off. Lift your arm into the air and, in a swooping arch, slam it down on the snooze button. Alternate the wake-up arm.

Shut off your alarm with your feet.

When the alarm goes off, snap up into a sitting position and yell, "Is that you Harry?" Men may yell, "Is that you Harriet?" If you know no Harriet, nor Harry, the exercise is still valid even if the names are not. You can use both names if you are really kinky.

Set your alarm in the next room.

When the alarm sounds, prop yourself up slowly on either the right or left elbow and say, "I'm not going to be able to make it through the day." Repeat this fifty to one hundred times. Then swing over to the other elbow, repeating, "I'm not going to make it through the day."

Right after the alarm goes off say out loud, "I'm going to do something about this crazy world today. I really mean it." Then slap your hand on your thigh, preferably while your hand is still under the covers.

Open your eyes. Don't just open your eyes, slam them open.

Open your eyes. Look quickly to the left and the right to see if the person you went to sleep with the night before is still with you. If it was a farm animal, try to get it out of the house without getting caught. Or, if you went to sleep alone, make certain that you are still alone.

 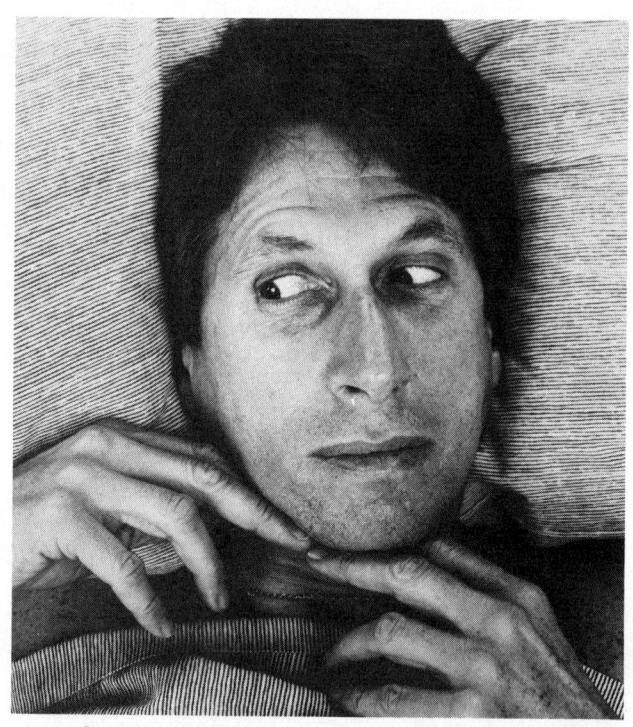

When getting out of bed, take the covers and sheets with you and roll towards the bathroom. This rolling exercise will stimulate all the muscles that are to be used that day—except for the brain. That will be stimulated when your head bumps against the bathroom door, which you will have purposely left closed the night before.

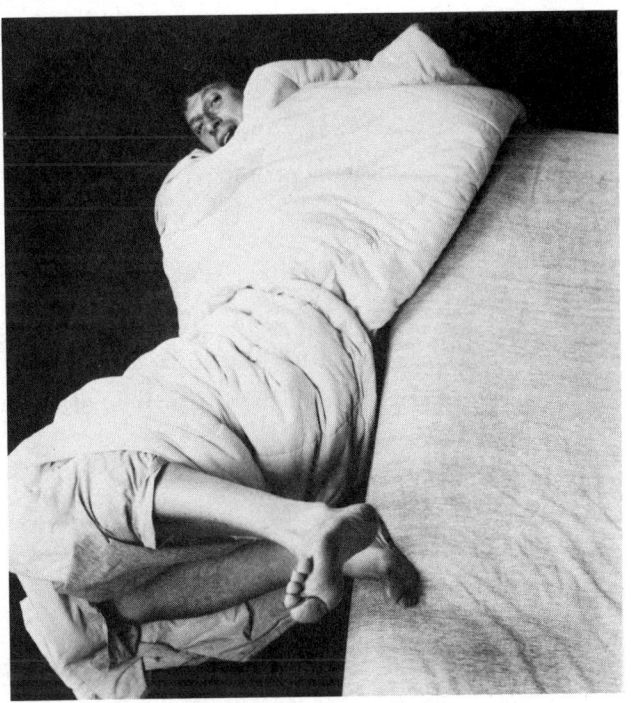

Make believe you are in someone else's bedroom and his or her spouse is entering. Jolting out of bed and then out of a room and/or a window is very good for the heart, liver, and ankles. Try to jolt whenever possible.

When you get out of bed, climb over the headboard.

Try to get out of the side of the bed that is against the wall.

The Bathroom

Pound on the bathroom door, screaming, "Hurry up in there. I have to get washed! I have to go to work! I'm going to be late! Are you going to be in there all day or what?" Do this even if you live alone and know that no one is in the bathroom. You are exercising your fist and at the same time stretching your vocal muscles.

If someone answers, press your ear against the door. This will exercise your lobes.

If the person who answers is unknown to you and should not be in your bathroom, immediately roll yourself back into the sheets and blankets and call the police. If you can't reach the phone, roll to the police station.

Walk like a real schlump into the bathroom: stoop-shouldered, stomach hanging, arms limp at your side, sheet trailing along the rug. Once in the bathroom straighten your spine, throw your shoulders back, lift your chin up, suck in your stomach, and look into the mirror. You haven't really done anything, but you look like you did. This is at least worth 90 percent of any exercise.

Keep a large scale in your bathroom. Every morning step over it on your way to the commode.

Stub your toe and scream, "Damn, damn, damn!" to exercise the jaw muscles. Also hopping around on one foot is a very good leg exercise.

18

When you stub your toe, jump around on one foot for several minutes. Switch to other foot and repeat.

The commode can be an extremely useful exercise tool. Lift the lid and the seat and sit down on the cold porcelain.

When flushing don't just use the old two-finger push; use both hands.

Cover the seat with a very furry or long shag rug cover. As you are performing your "duty," the cover will be too thick, causing the seat to plunge downward. The move you make to save the precious part of your life is a fantastic exercise and one at which you will never fail. However, if you do fail, you won't have to exercise ever again; you won't have anything to live for anyway. Should this happen, you will have to use the same exercises, indicated for the female.

When you go to the bathroom, try to keep the lid up with one foot, if you are a man. If you are a woman, try to keep the lid *down* with one foot.

While you are sitting on the cold toilet seat, do a lift-off with both hands. Repeat.

Comb your hair with a one-tooth comb.

When flossing teeth, hold floss stationary and move your head.

Try to get the toothpaste out of the tube, with the cap on.

Use the wrong end of your toothbrush.

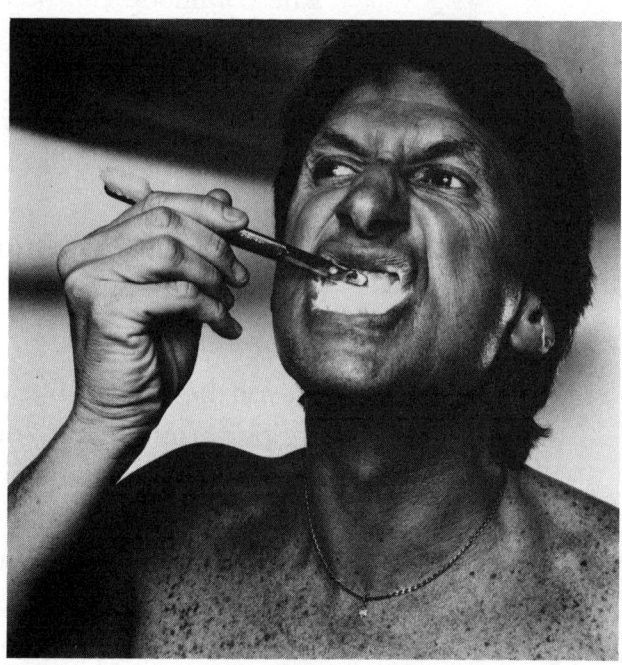

Keep a very, very small bar of soap that slips out of your hand so you have to stoop to find it.

Turn on the shower without using your hands.

Turn yourself on without using your hands.

Soap the bottom of your bathtub.

Put your towel on the floor and roll around on it to dry.

Shave with a kitchen knife.

Variation: Shave with a tweezer.

While showering think of the famous scene from the movie *Psycho*. Then have someone suddenly whip open the curtain and plunge a fake knife or a banana into your chest.

When taking a shower, suddenly turn the cold water off. The steaming burst of hot water will make you leap from the tub. Variation: turn off the hot water.

Squat thrusts are important. Get into a hot tub—as hot as you can stand it. You will be up and down eight or nine times, easily.

Slap on your aftershave lotion with both hands simultaneously.

Get into a fight with your wife or girl friend and then have her slap on your aftershave lotion for you.

Steam the bathroom mirror so you have to squint to see your image while you are shaving.

Do not plug in the hair dryer, but go through all the motions until your hair is dry.

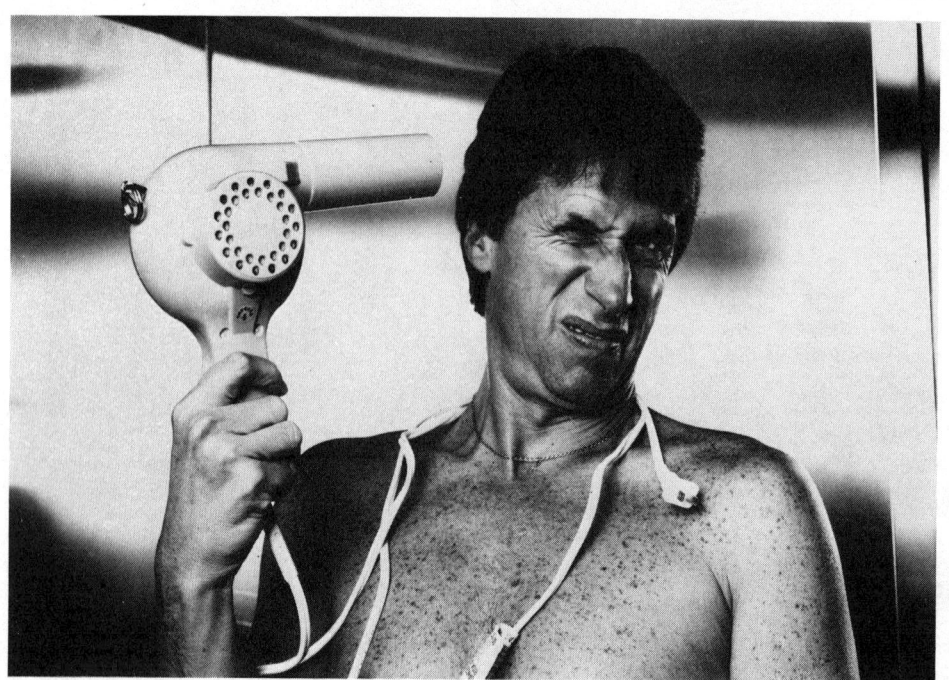

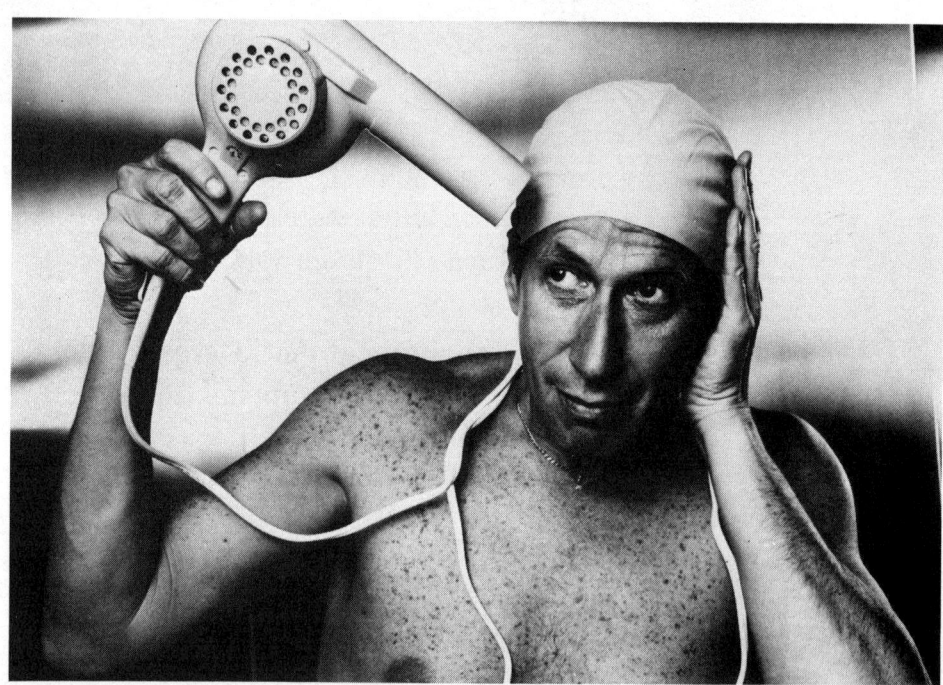

If you are bald, blow-dry your head. Then go through brush-and-comb motions as though you had a full head of hair.

Sing an aria from any opera at the top of your lungs. When your neighbor starts to pound on the wall, pound back.

Blow your nose four times, as hard as you can. Then lift your hands up from your sides and get a tissue.

Put on your deodorant without lifting up your arms. If you use a roll-on deodorant, insert the ball under your arm and try to roll it around without using the other hand.

Getting Dressed

Get dressed underneath the covers.

Place your underwear on the floor. Slip each foot into the leg openings. Lie down on your back, put your legs up in the air, let your underwear slide down to your pelvic area. How you get it up to your waist is up to you.

Keep your underwear in the freezer.

Wear underwear with a stretched-out elastic waistband. Putting your hands in your pants to pull up your underwear is good exercise.

Close the hooks of your bra. Step into it and pull it up over your body into position. Then slip your arms through.

Another good exercise is to put your bra on backward so the back strap is in the front. Walk around a few minutes wearing it this way. Look in the mirror. Laughter is good for the abdominal muscles. NOTE: If you put on your bra backward and it fits, you know it is going to be a bad day, especially if it also fits in the back. NOTE: Women can also do these bra exercises (probably better).

Put on pantyhose that are at least five sizes too small. Pretend they are the right size.

When you have time for a quick exercise, pull on knee-high pantyhose and try to stretch them up to your crotch.

Put your pants on with the belt already buckled.

Put your pants on only up to the knees and tighten the belt. Now act like you are in a hurry. Falling is very good for testing one's agility.

Try to get on a pair of designer jeans in less than five minutes.

Try to get them off.

Purposely leave your fly open. Spend the entire day and evening like this once a week. Every time a person tells you that your fly is open, put one hand up to your cheek in utter embarrassment, using the other to grab the zipper and pull it up quickly. Do this as often as possible prior to actual arrest.

Put on a new pair of socks without first removing the staple. Now walk around.

Put your hands through the holes in your pants pockets and try to pull up your socks.

Put both feet in one sock and see how long you can keep your balance.

When putting on your socks, stand instead of sit. Try to avoid crashing into the furniture.

Put both socks on one foot. Take them off and put both socks on the other foot.

Put one stocking on one of your feet, put the other stocking over your head. Put a ghetto blaster on your shoulder. Make believe you are making a getaway from a bank.

Tie your shoelaces together. Shuffling is good exercise, but you must remember to untie the laces before driving to work.

Let both your shoelaces remain undone. Every time someone mentions it you can look down quickly.

Take your shoes off while they are still tied.

Try to kick the pennies out of your penny loafers.

Fasten all the buttons, the sleeves, and the front of your shirt and then put your shirt on.

Use only one hand to tie your necktie. Use the other hand to untie it.

Perform this exercise with a clip-on bow tie.

Button your suit jacket first and then put it on.

The hat should be put on first thing in the morning and all other clothing should be put on after. This is especially effective if one wears a turtleneck sweater.

Wear your underwear for two straight weeks. Then try to get out of it.

Every week buy a garment with a larger waist size, and then show your friends how well you are doing on your David Brenner Exercise Program by sticking your thumbs in the waistband and pulling it out while saying, "Look at all this!"

Meals at Home

Boil yourself two three-minute eggs and eat them with a fork, trying to keep the slimy stuff balanced on your fork. For advanced students, leave eggs in their shells.

Put two slices of bread in the toaster without plugging the toaster into the wall. Tap your foot impatiently. Alternate feet.

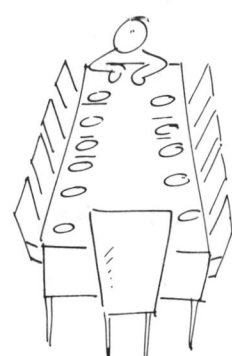

Set your breakfast table for twelve and then eat alone.

Pretend your are Jimmy Cagney and stuff a half grapefruit in someone's face. Now remember who you really are and run. Variation: Use a whole grapefruit.

Fill in the holes in the salt and pepper shakers, but don't give up trying to use them on your food.

Using four fingers and a thumb, flatten each strip of bacon.

Pour some cereal into a big bowl and eat it dry without a spoon.

To accompany your eggs, eat a frozen steak—without a knife.

Eat a peanut butter sandwich without drinking anything.

Make a very big sandwich to take with you to work, for lunch. Make another one. Make another one. Make another one. Make another one . . .

While waiting for food to warm in the oven, run in place. You may even get good enough to try this without a microwave.

Place some food on the floor for a dog or some other pet you don't have. Realizing your mistake, bend down and eat on all fours like a dog. Advanced students should eliminate the dog dish.

Make a big pizza, but instead of cutting the slices, divide them by hand.

Eat oatmeal with chopsticks.

Try to open a canned ham without a key.

Housework

When opening any drawer, make believe it is stuck. Use both hands and fake exertion.

Before leaving the house every morning, make up your bed. Just sheets, blankets, pillowcases—no mattress.

Lightly grease all the doorknobs in your house.

Add extra stairs to your staircase.

Press your clothes without plugging in the iron.

Don't buy insecticides; go after the bugs manually.

Use a manual can opener. Keep the can still and walk around it.

Try to seal a Tupperware bowl with one hand.

Lean against an agitating washing machine.

Rent a shampooer and try to do the carpet yourself.

Try to straighten the piece of Saran Wrap using one hand.

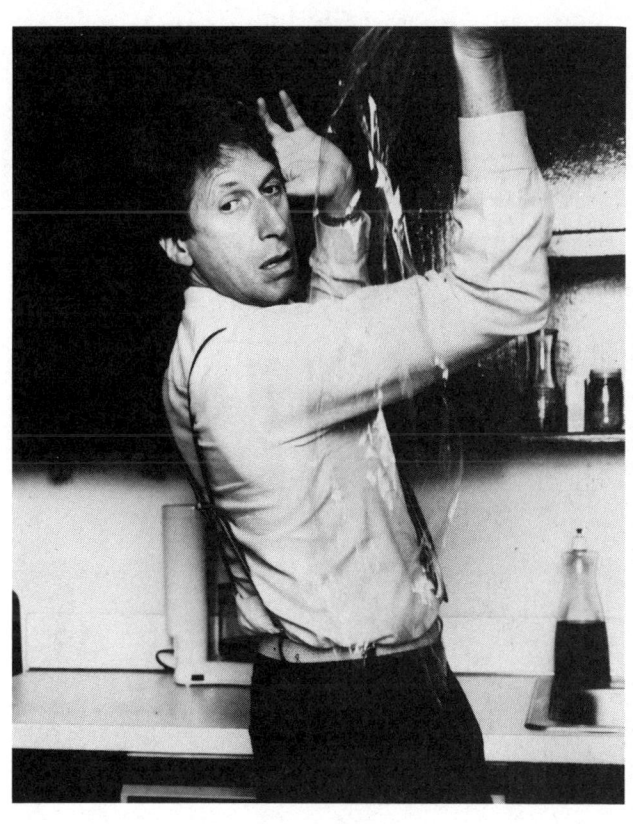
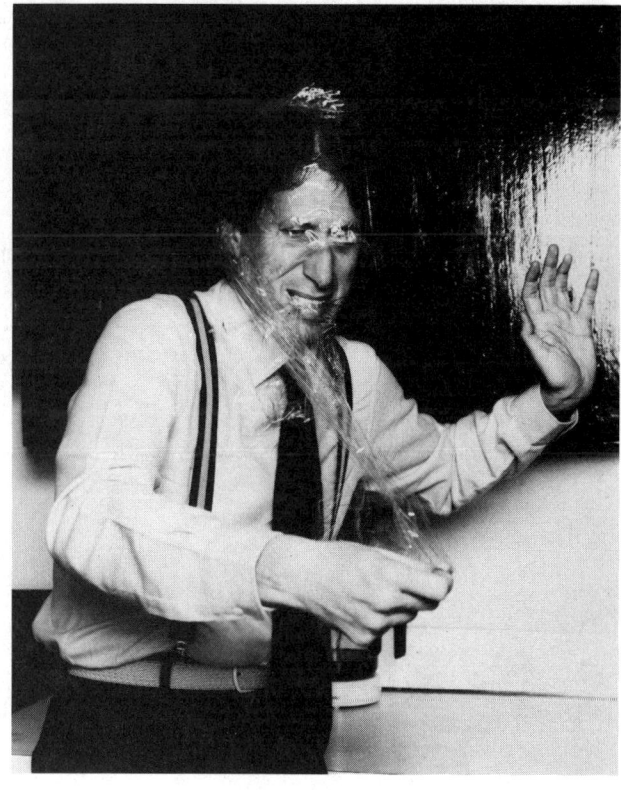

Rip Saran Wrap without using the edge of the box.

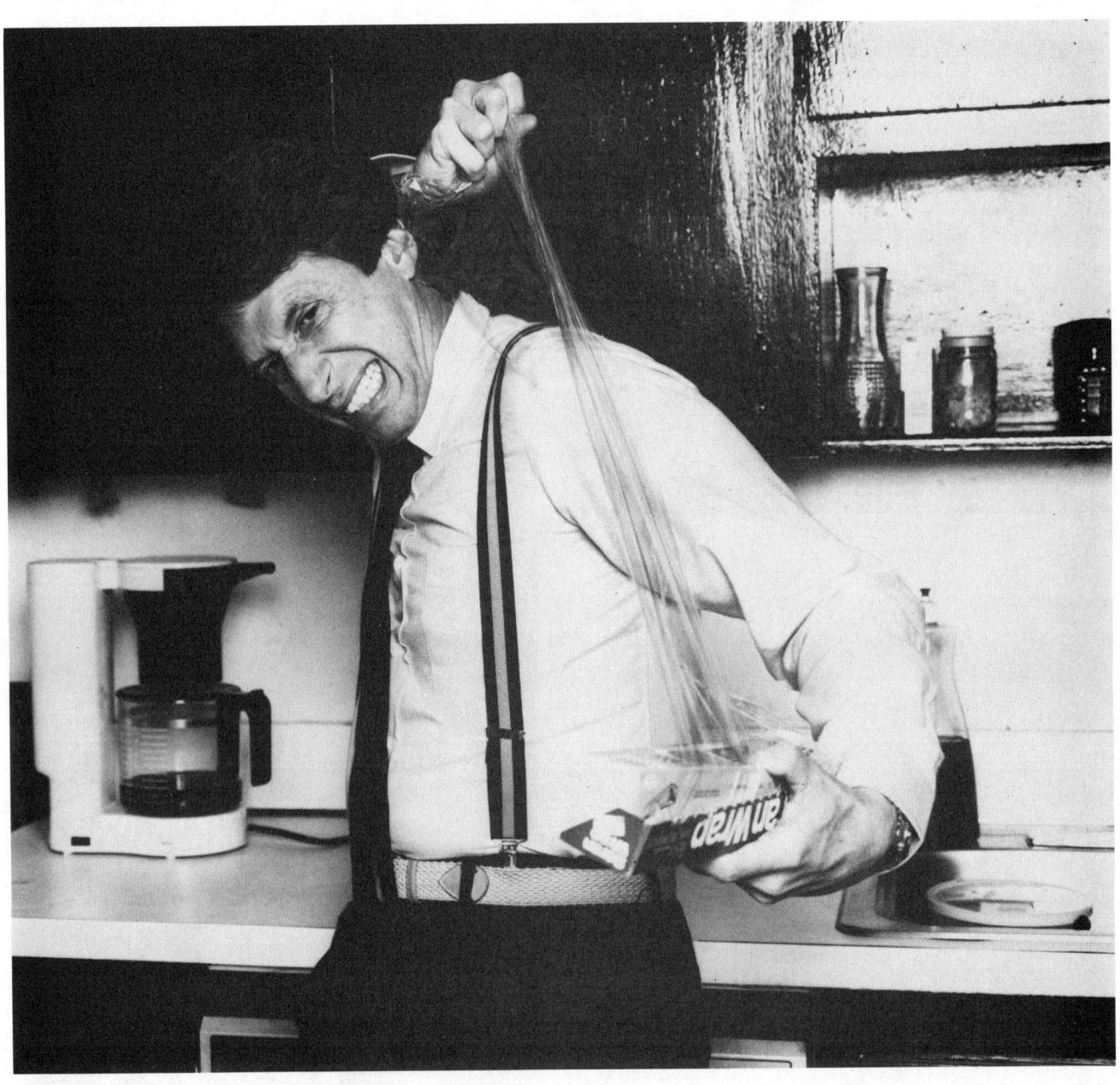

Shopping

Shop at a supermarket that doesn't have automatic opening doors.

Use a shopping cart with locked wheels.

Try to separate the shopping carts that are stuck together.

When charging something, volunteer to work the charge machine.

Driving to Work

Buy an American-made car. Lifting the hood constantly is good for building upper-body strength.

Back your car out of the garage and driveway while sitting in the back seat.

Wear your seat belt at all times, even when getting out of the car.

Make believe you are a chain smoker and constantly push in your cigarette lighter. Alternate the fingers so that each one gets exercise.

Make believe you have children in the back seat who are annoying you. Keep turning around and screaming, "I told you, you should have gone to the bathroom before you left the house! Stop putting that in your mouth! Don't do that to your sister! Leave the dog alone!"

When someone is in the car with you, make sharp turns and try to stay on your side of the seat.

Once a month leave the car at home and take the bus to work. When you arrive at the office, call the bus company and tell them where you left their bus.

If you drive a car with automatic transmission, go through the motions of shifting gears.

Make believe your car is a convertible and try to get the roof down.

While taking your car through an automatic car wash, sit on the hood or roof.

Make believe your car doors are stuck. Enter and exit through the windows.

Adjust your car seat forward and backward, forward and backward. Take a deep breath. Repeat. When you feel you have enough stamina, try this exercise with a fat person sitting next to you.

Make believe you are an elderly person. Sink very low in the seat and peek just a little bit over the steering wheel.

See how many pairs of gloves you can stuff in your glove compartment.

Rotate your hubcaps every other day.

Attach your necktie to the windshield wipers. Put them on at full speed. Advanced students: attach your neck.

Remove the front seat from your car and continue driving.

When putting change in the toll basket don't just drop it in. Get out of the car and make some moves!

During an eclipse of the sun, get out of your car and shadow-box.

Pull up behind a parked, empty vehicle. Make believe the driver has just violated a driving rule and caused you great distress. Remove your seat belt frantically, leap out of your car, race up to his, pound on his door, yell and scream, wave your arms in the air, get back in your car, screech backward, pull out, and drive off quickly.

If you always park in the same lot at work, beat the attendant to the job by kicking a dent in the fender on your own.

Go to the Department of Motor Vehicles for a problem with a simple solution. Being sent to different windows all day is good exercise.

Elevators and Escalators

Get off the elevator in your office building two or three floors before yours and walk to the other elevator.

Whenever an elevator stops at a floor, make believe it is an emergency stop and go into a crouched position. Act startled.

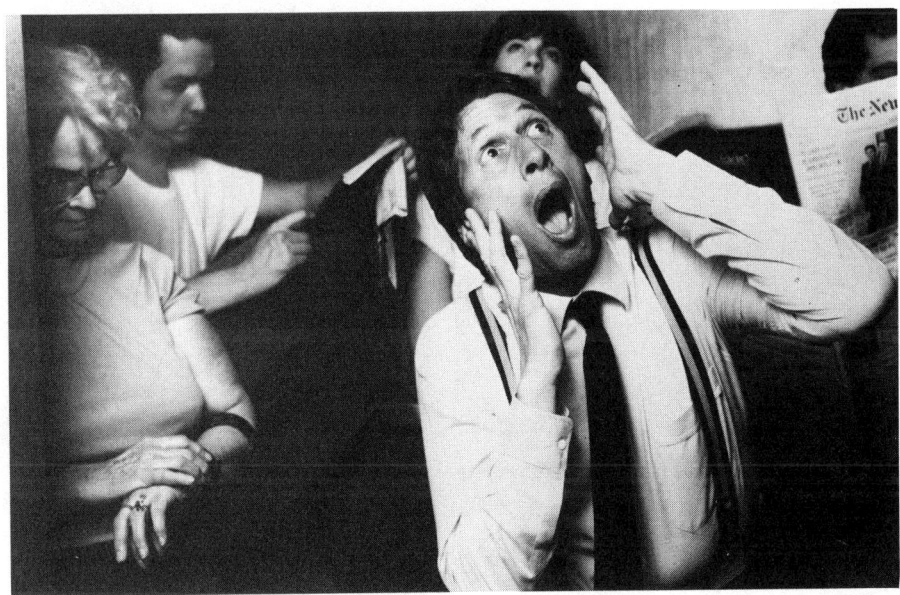

When a very, very fat person gets on the elevator, point to the line that reads "capacity" and the inspection chart and then try to push him or her out.

If your office building has an escalator, ride it the wrong way. Go up the down steps and down the up steps.

Take a long walk in the elevator.

Running is good exercise. If you have a choice between the escalator or the stairs, run to the escalator.

43

The Office

When throwing away your cup at the water cooler, challenge another employee to a quick game of one on one.

Use different parts of your anatomy to dial or to answer the phone.

Use your knuckles to operate a pushbutton phone.

Stretching is important. When the phone rings at the office, reach for it without taking your feet off the desk.

Develop good leg tone by getting a chair with wheels on it and rolling yourself around *everywhere*.

Sharpen your pencils with a spoon.

Put a heavier spring in your ballpoint pen.

Open your mail with your teeth.

Get coffee for the office staff and carry three cups in each hand.

When mixing a drink for your boss, jump up and down.

Point to a co-worker, yelling, "Visible panty lines, visible panty lines!" Ducking, running, and weaving are very good exercises. Also try this on women.

Read all your business papers upside down.

Turn the pages with your tongue.

Mimick your boss by jumping up and down on your desk, making funny faces, crossing your eyes, and yelling, "Merger, merger!" Hunting for work is good exercise.

Never mark the page where you have left off. This way you will have to search through the book to find your place.

When reading, keep your eyes still and move the book.

When you leave the office, hail a cab at rush hour. Walking is good for you.

When speaking on the phone, cradle both parts of the phone under your chin.

While on the phone, skip rope with the cord. If you have a cordless phone use your imagination.

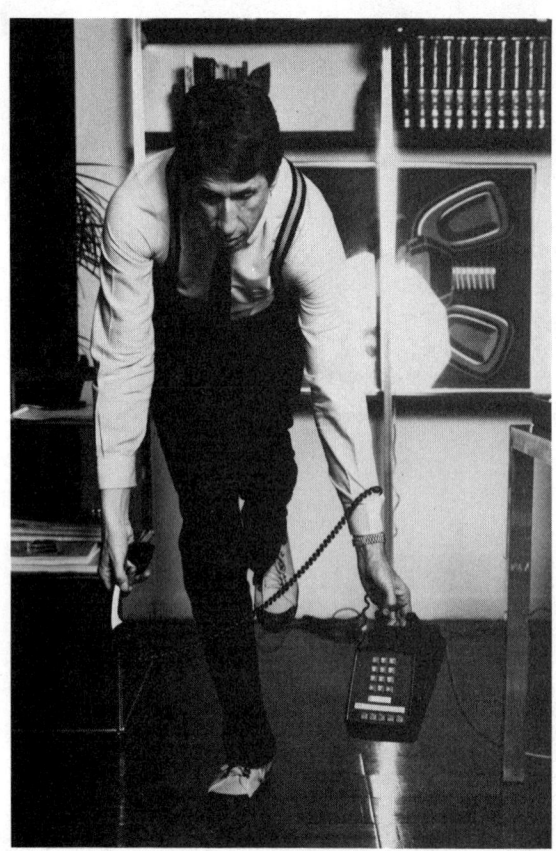

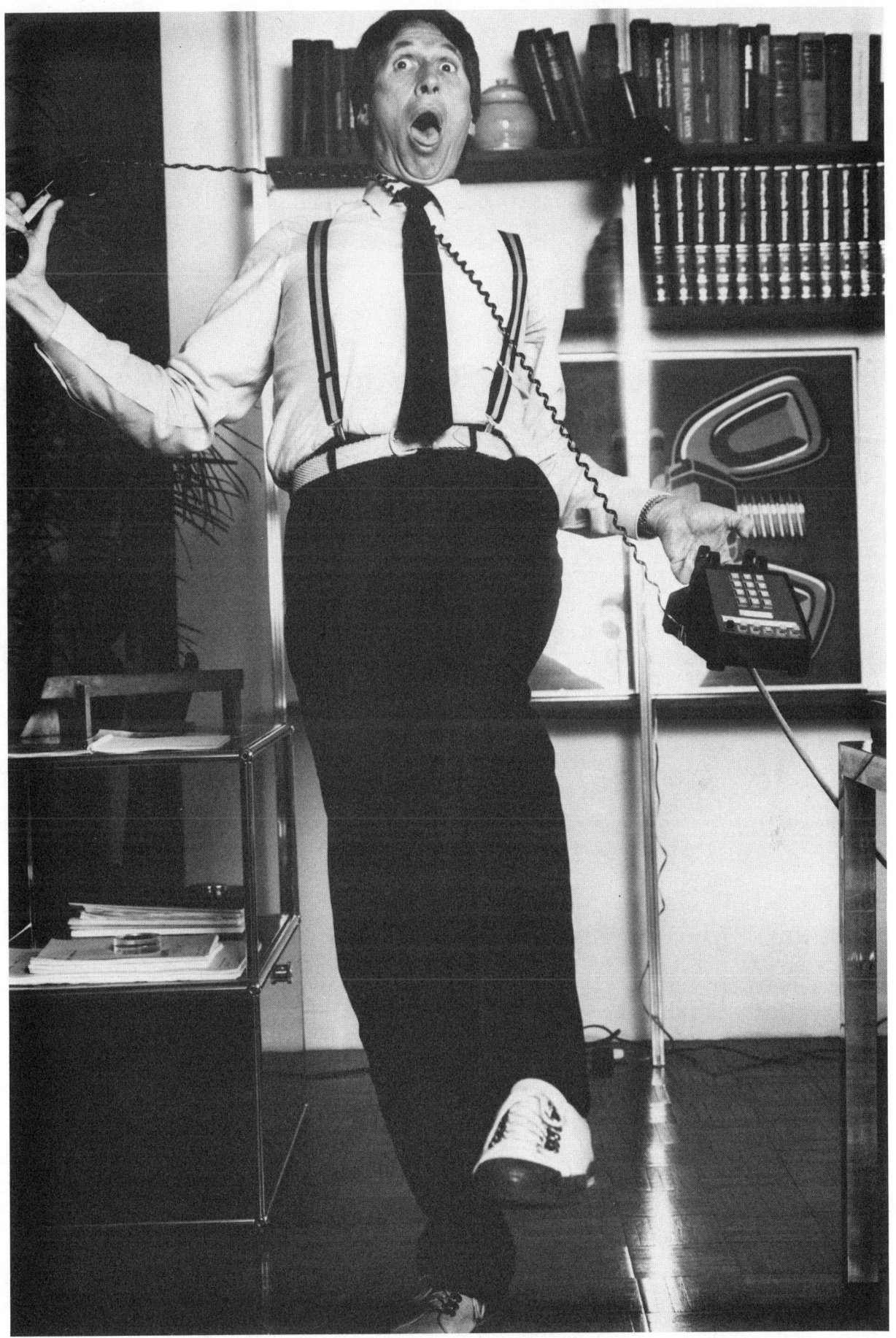

Turn the pages by blowing on them.

When talking to a co-worker who is seated at his or her desk while you are standing, lean on the desk with one hand and then quickly shift to the other hand. Continue this until the conversation ends. Do two more pushoffs for good luck.

At conference meetings always make believe you have to go to the bathroom. Raise your hand and ask permission first and then stand. Sit down and repeat.

Use a one-inch ruler and a quarter-inch-long pencil.

Leave your reminder notes on a paper 18 by 24 inches, then fold it up into wallet size and place it in your pocket.

When asked to get coffee for co-workers, carry them over to the coffee machine or cart.

Press your intercom with your nose. Try different parts of the body.

Make believe you have a window in your office and try to open it.

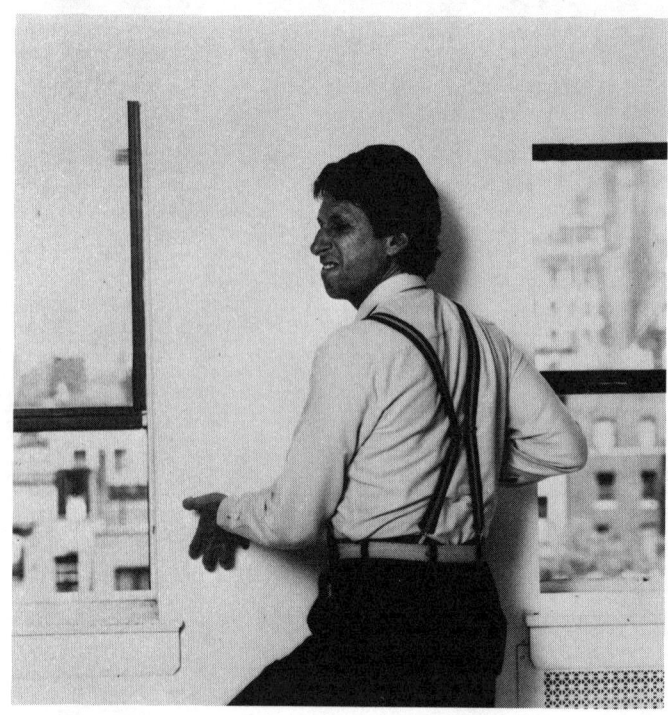

If you have the kind of a job where you must wear many different hats, wear them all at the same time.

Punch a hole in the bottom of a cup, fill with water at the cooler, and then try to get back to your desk before it's empty. For advanced students: try to get to someone else's desk.

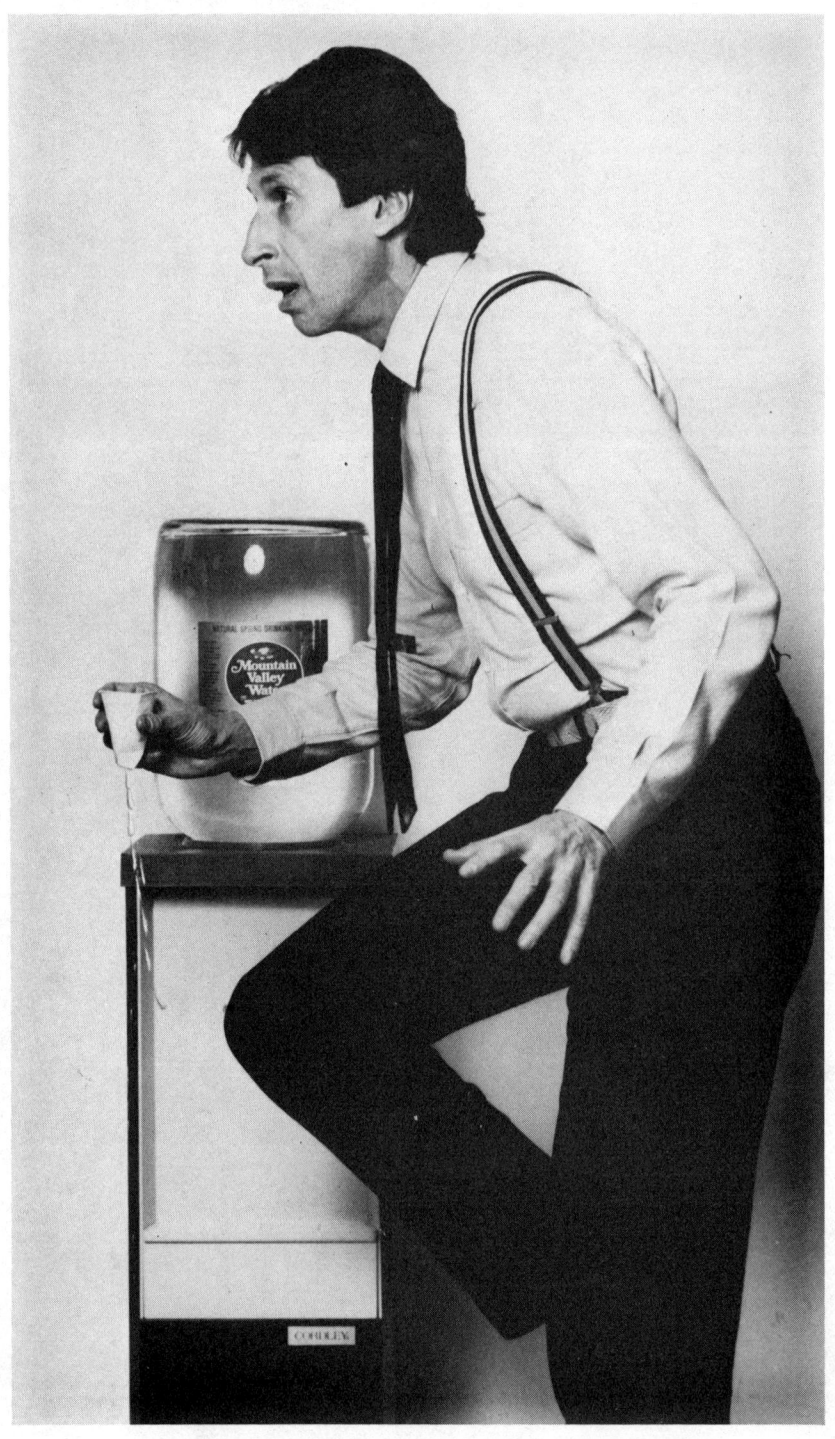

Conversation

At least six times a day, while someone is telling you a boring story, act as though you are shocked by throwing your mouth open and slapping your cheek with your open palm. Utter various exclamations, for example, "I don't believe it! You must be kidding!" "Not in a million years!" "You actually said that?"

While listening to a story do a few southern-style "Well, I'll be's." At the same time, lift either leg and slap your hand between knee and thigh.

When emphasizing a point, poke the person in the chest or shoulder. Use a different finger and your thumb with each poke. Then use your other hand. Now bend the fingers and poke with your knuckles. Then take off your shoes and poke with your toes.

When laughing, no matter how hard, throw your head back. Stay in this position until something not funny is said and then return to the upright stance.

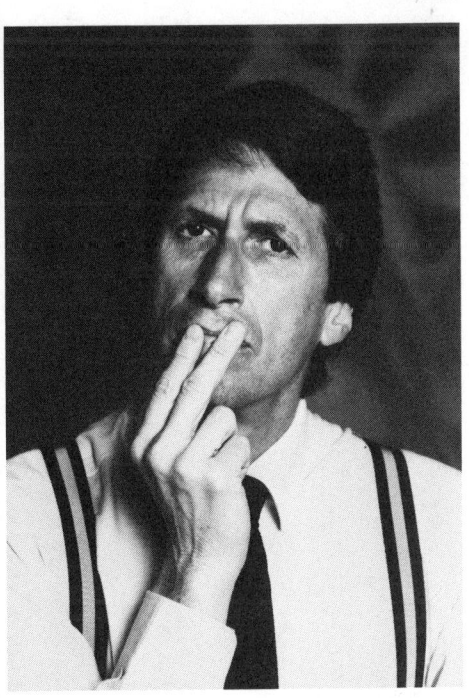 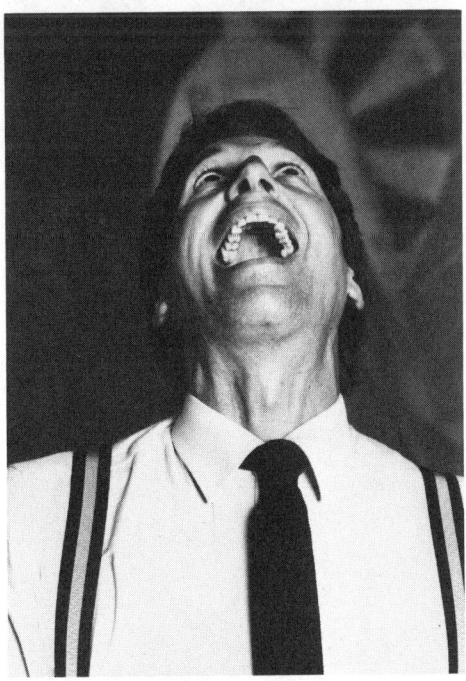 

If you hear your name spoken, no matter how softly, spin around as if you were frightened.

When being introduced to someone, make at least six aborted attempts to shake his or her hand.

At least once a day make up a story about a large bird and flap your arms up and down in a demonstration of what the bird looked like. An alternative to this is a giraffe story for the neck muscles, a gorilla story for the back muscles, a cute little mouse story for those itsy, bitsy, cutesy, eensy, teensy, little tips of the toe muscles.

When listening to someone, keep cupping your ears as if you are hard of hearing. Increase the cupping motion speed.

When in conversation, interrupt the speaker with the statement "Wait a minute; let's see what the person over there thinks about this." Then walk across the street or across the room or halfway down the block and make believe you are talking to someone. Return and say, "He didn't know" or "He had no opinion." Let the other person continue talking.

Every so often when you are talking to someone, walk around the person three or four times.

Back up rapidly and then return to the starting position.

Try to work Jerry Lewis into the conversation. Then do an impression of him.

When you talk to short people pick them up to speak to them.

Respond to someone's conversation by saying, "I *love* it!" and then do a little dance.

Make believe everyone you talk to is at least a foot taller than you.

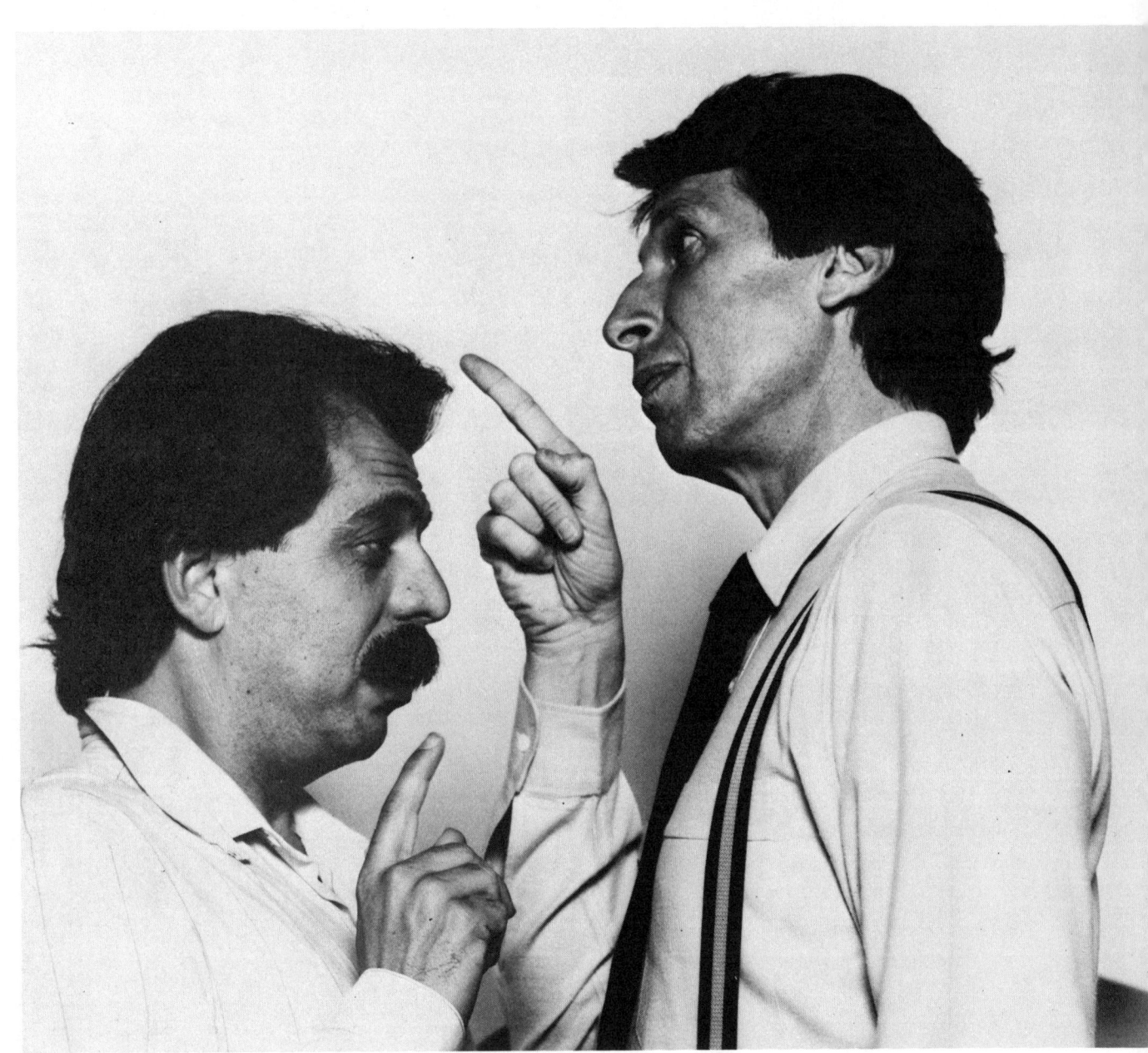

Find someone who talks to himself in public. Walk around with him all day and pretend you are having a conversation.

Dining Out

Take a slow walk to a nearby greasy spoon. After you eat try not to run back to your office.

Try to open up the little packets of soup crackers or the ketchup and mustard packets without using your teeth.

When you pick bones from a fish try to reconstruct the skeleton.

When drinking, set the glass down and tip the table.

When you suck up a milkshake, first pinch the straw in three places.

When you taste wine in a restaurant, gargle.

When salting food, hold the shaker with the holes on the top.

When you eat spaghetti, hold the fork still and twirl the dish.

Twirl spaghetti with a fork. Don't be afraid of this exercise; have a second plate.

62

Eat spaghetti by sucking one strand at a time.

BACKGROUND ART BY SIMON SCUDERA

Go into the kitchen and try to get the chef to wear a hair net—on his arms, too!

Go to McDonald's and refuse to leave until they add your burger to their sign of the number served.

Try the Heimlich maneuver on someone, especially if he is not choking. Then put him down and run.

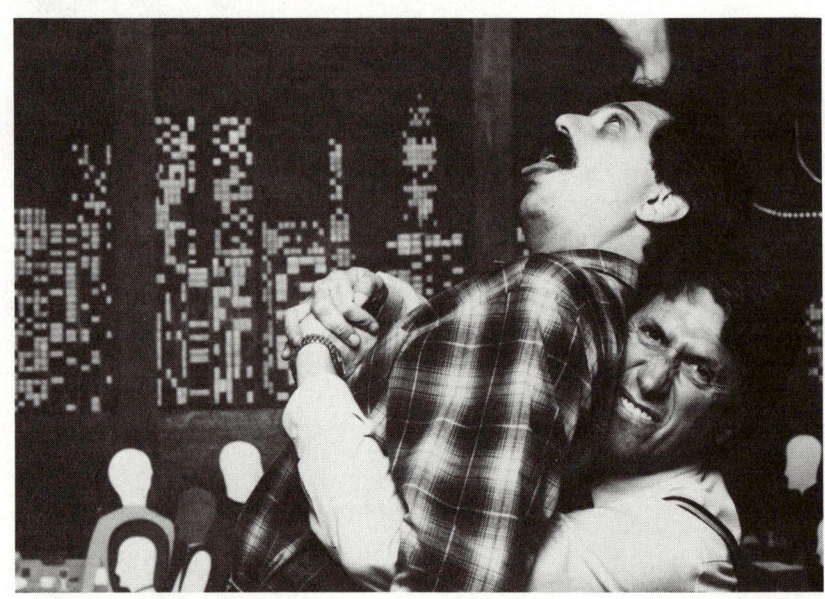

U se a fork to eat soup.

Ethnic Exercises

Go to a Greek restaurant. Tell the counterman you want a lamb shish kebab, but you want to slice the lamb yourself. Don't use a knife.

Go to a Japanese restaurant. Bow in greeting. Bow again. Bow again. Bow again. Bow again. Bow again . . .

Go to a Mexican restaurant. Eat and then run back to the office.

Go to a Mexican restaurant and yell, "Border Patrol."

Go to an Italian restaurant. Set off a firecracker and charge out unnoticed with everyone else.

Go to a Polish restaurant. Keep moving around until you have read the insignia on everyone's bowling shirt.

Go to a Polish restaurant and keep your fingers in the bowling ball while you eat.

Go to a German restaurant. Wear a large Star of David outside your shirt and feel the tension tightening up your muscles.

Go to a Kosher deli. Hold up your corned beef sandwich and yell, "You call this lean?"

Go to an Arab restaurant. Sit with your legs folded underneath you and leave the same way.

Go to a Chinese restaurant and bring laundry.

Go to a Chinese restaurant and use only one chopstick.

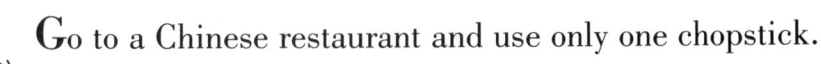

Go to a soul food restaurant with a white hood over your head and a white sheet covering your body.

Go to a Cuban restaurant and try to get everyone to act out the restaurant-shootout scene from the movie *Scarface*.

Go to a sushi bar and complain vigorously that everything is undercooked.

Look for a good Phoenician restaurant.

Dancing

Go to the hottest discotheque. Dance as hard as you can. When the doors open continue dancing.

Disco dance to an entire Lawrence Welk album.

When they play a romantic slow dance, do the bunny hop.

Enter a waltz contest and wear shoes with very thick rubber-crepe soles and heels.

Go to your local country and western bar and dance hall. Ask the biggest most macho-looking guy to dance. This only applies to men. (Then again maybe it will be as much exercise for women.)

Slow dance with a fat person and try to dip him or her.

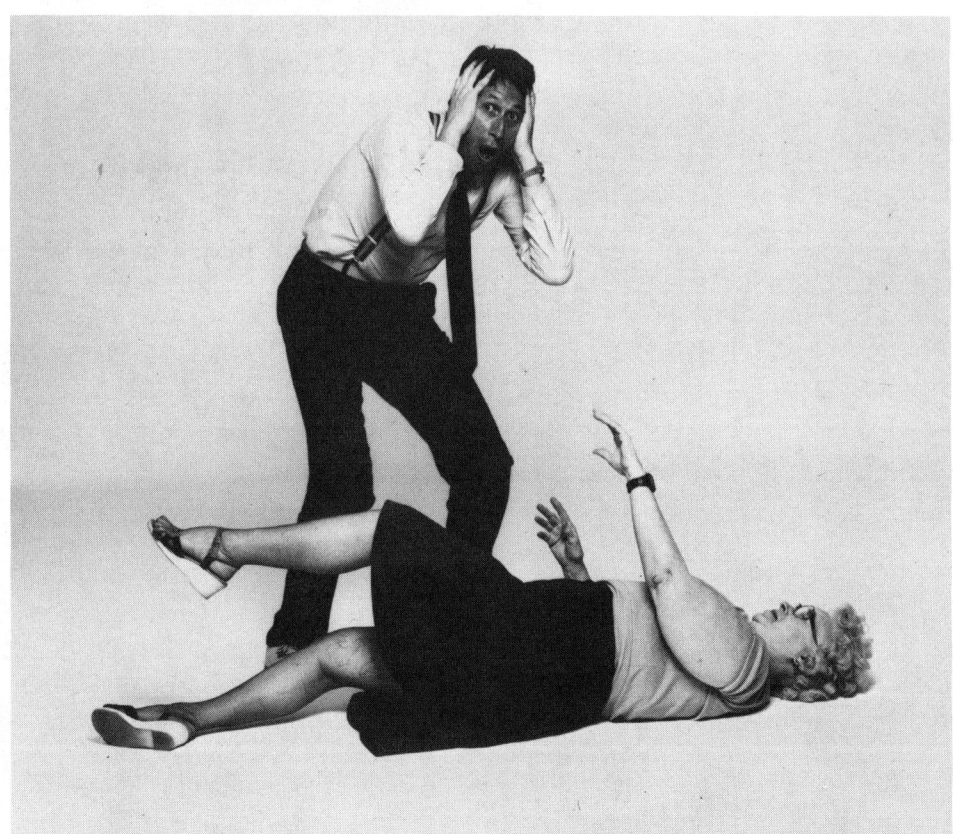

Sex

Go at it full blast as you have never done it before. Spend at least an hour in the bedroom. Then call up your date and invite her over. Try to repeat the performance when she gets there.

Both parties get on top simultaneously.

Have a discussion when you make love.

Put a mirror on the ceiling and have sex on the floor.

Put a mirror on the floor and have sex on the ceiling.

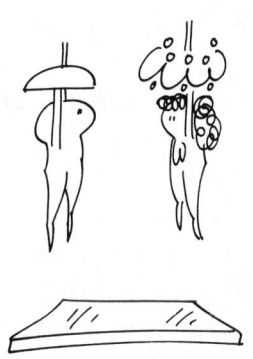

Calorie Chart

It is a well-known fact that sexual activity uses up calories. The following chart will help you determine how many calories you use during different sexual acts, each about thirty minutes long. If you spend only fifteen minutes divide the number of calories by half. If you spend an hour multiply the number by two. If it takes you five hours to complete this, write to the *Guinness Book of World Records*.

	Calories Per Half Hour
Sex with a spouse of more than fifty years	7
Sex with a spouse of more than twenty-five years	10
Sex with a spouse of five to twenty-five years	12
Sex with a spouse of more than one year but less than five	25
Sex with a spouse of one year	35
Sex on a honeymoon with a spouse	150
Sex on a honeymoon with someone other than your spouse	350
Sex with someone else's spouse on his or her honeymoon	750
Sex with someone else's spouse on his or her honeymoon and getting caught	1000
Sex with someone else's spouse on his or her honeymoon, getting caught, and then having sex with the person who caught you	2500
Sex with someone you have been dating one to three years	400
Sex with someone you have been dating a month	600
Sex with someone you have been dating a week	700
Sex with someone you have been dating a day	800
Sex with someone you've been dating a day who looks like Doris Day	825
Sex with someone you've been dating a day who looks like Dennis Day	875
Sex with someone you have been dating an hour	900
Sex with someone you have been dating three minutes	1200
Sex with three people you've been dating one minute	1500
Sex with someone you have just met (within the first minute of meeting)	1700
Sex by yourself	100
Sex in front of your pet	50
If your pet is a gorilla	100
Sex <u>with</u> your gorilla	14,000
Sex with a Jewish girl	see sex by yourself

Calorie Consumption by Sexual Position

There are a number of additional calories to be burned away while having sex for a half hour. The same scale ratio that applies to the previous chart applies to this. Simply add the additional calorie losses to the amount already deducted.

Position	Calories
Missionary position	20
Missionary position with a missionary	1200
Doggie position	50
Doggie position with a doggie	400
Doggie position with a missionary	600
On floor covered by rug	75
On floor made of wood	100
On floor of stone or brick	140
On floor of stainless steel	600
On roof of a building	85
On a hot tin roof	200
With a cat on a hot tin roof	250
Against the wall	50
Against the ceiling	5000
On a sofa	75
Under the sofa	750
While one person is on the sofa and one person is under the sofa	1000
On a chair	20
With a chair	220
On a table	80
On a table containing food and plates	400
On a table containing food, plates and persons eating	850
On the street	80
In the street	180
Against a tree	60
In a tree	600
Falling out of a tree	6000
While climbing a tree	7000
In a hammock that's tied to only one tree	400
In a folding chair that keeps folding	550
In a phone booth	350
Outside a phone booth	375
In a phone booth while someone's outside the phone booth	400
With Shirley Booth	425
While making a long-distance call	450

Holidays

One of the best times to get yourself in shape is a holiday season, although it is rarely considered so by "experts" in the exercise, dieting, and physical fitness fields. These are times when we partake in once-a-year activities; therefore our minds and bodies are conditioned to accept new experiences. So why not broaden those experiences during the holidays to include unique and fun ways of becoming physically fit, toning up, peeling off those extra pounds, tightening up, getting rid of old flab city, and generally just looking good!

Presidents' Day—Abraham Lincoln

Buy a black suit that would fit a man 6'5". If you are 6'5", buy a suit that would fit a man 6'10". If you are 6'10" buy a suit that would fit a man 7'5", and so forth through 18'5". Then you must put on the suit and keep it looking like it fits you all day. Keep pulling the pants up as you walk and as you sit. Keep pulling the sleeves back so that they fit. Tighten up the shoulders. If you get compliments on how well you look, how well you're dressed, you'll know that you are performing this exercise perfectly.

Go to a theater in your community. Sit in a box seat and constantly whip around to catch John Wilkes Booth about to assassinate you.

Split some rails.

Take a regular-size envelope and try to copy the entire Gettysburg Address on it.

If you do not feel like wearing the entire Abraham Lincoln garb, just try the stovepipe hat. You will be ducking constantly throughout the day and evening.

Eat Stove Top Stuffing while wearing a stovepipe hat.

Eat Stove Top Stuffing out of a stovepipe hat.

Dress in full Abraham Lincoln garb. Go into a run-down store in a bad neighborhood. Select a clerk, preferably of a minority background. Announce that you are Abraham Lincoln and you are freeing him and try to remove him from the store.

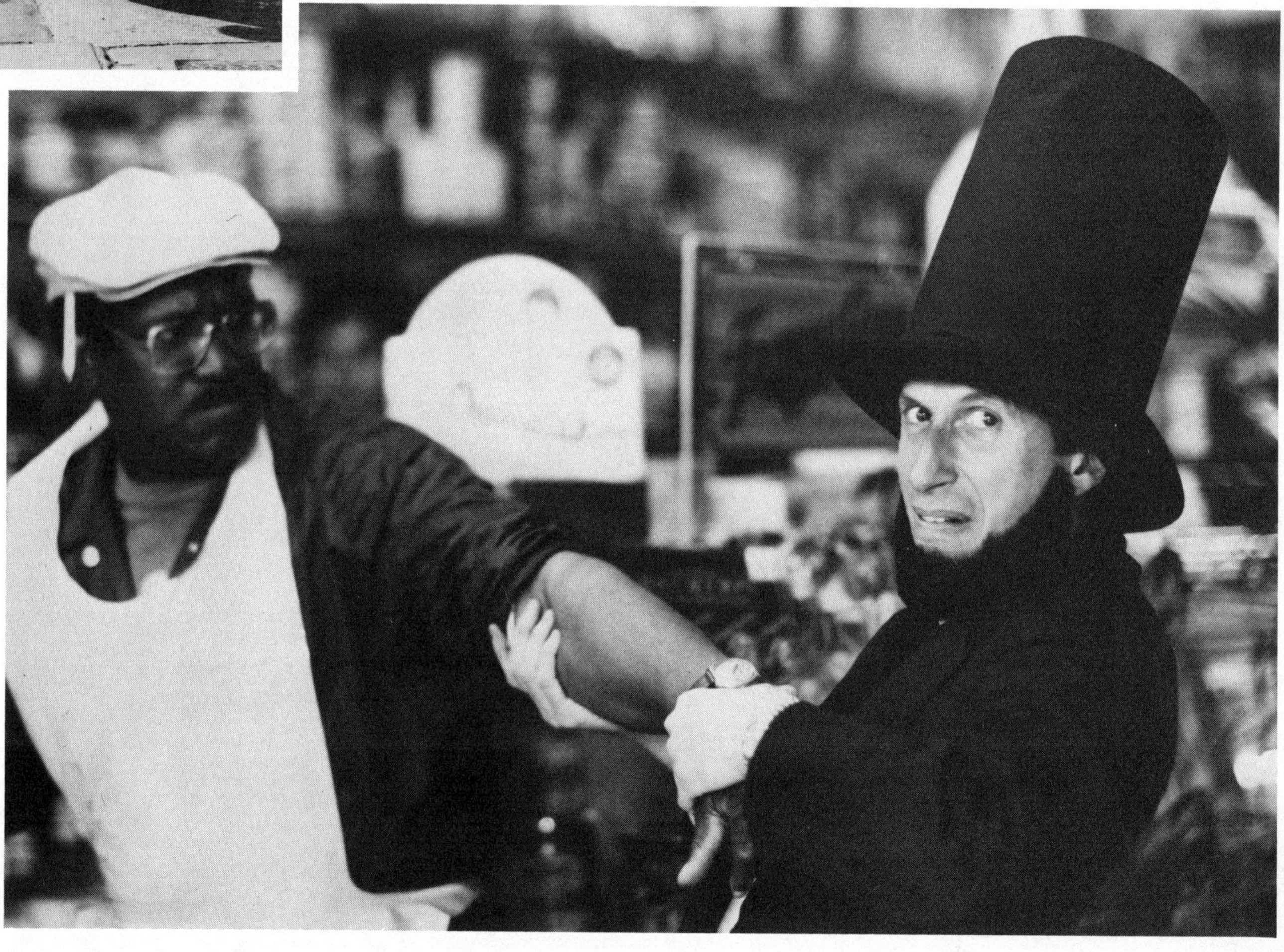

If successful you will be proud and can repeat the exercise. If unsuccessful buy *Exercises You Can Do in A Body Cast*.

Presidents' Birthdays— George Washington

Chop down your neighbor's tree. Deny it.

Wear tight pants and a powdered wig to a truck stop.

Make a list of as many black athletes as you can who are named Washington.

Go to a local sporting shop and try standing up inside a rowboat for the hour it took George Washington to cross the Delaware River.

Go to your local woodcraft shop and have a pair of false teeth made for you. Wear them.

Try making out while wearing the wooden teeth.

For extra exercise you can polish the wooden teeth, preferably while they are still in your mouth.

Wear a white wig and carry a dollar bill in your pocket. Take it out for everyone you see and point to it. Smile and say, "That's me!"

Ask your local butcher to let you into his freezer. Make believe the chickens are your troops in the snow of Valley Forge. Wrap their feet and your feet in old cloth. Pace up and down trying to figure out how to get into Philadelphia for a good cheese-steak or hoagie sandwich.

St. Patrick's Day

With orange in the St. Patrick's Day Parade.

Pick up all the empty beer cans and whiskey bottles on Fifth Avenue and the Upper East Side of Manhattan after the parade.

Pick up all the drunk's on Fifth Avenue.

Easter

Have a big egg roll and egg hunt on your lawn. Use raw eggs instead of hard-boiled.

Buy a male and female rabbit. Bring them home. Do everything they do for one week.

Break tradition by painting live chickens instead of eggs.

You might even have a chicken hunt or live chicken roll contest.

Go to church dressed as the Easter rabbit.

Passover

Instead of the traditional hiding of the piece of matzo in your house, have someone hide the matzo somewhere in the neighborhood and look for it. For more excitement, hide it in an Arab neighborhood.

At the ceremonial part of the dinner where you break the matzo, keep it in the box when you do it.

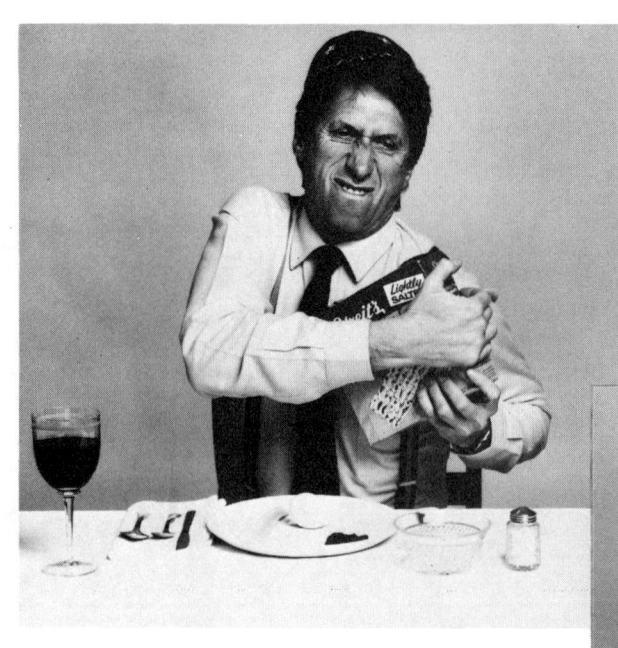

Serve a large Passover dinner without inviting anyone else. Don't eat the food, but keep changing seats and holding conversations. Take the flower centerpiece home with you.

Invite your friends over for a Passover egg or matzo brei hunt on your lawn.

Mother's Day

If you are a man, dress up as a woman and go out and complain all day about how nobody remembered you on your special day.

Spend the day on the subways and buses and count how many old ladies you see with their legs open.

Hide your mother or someone else's mother on your lawn and have everyone hunt for her.

Invite everyone over for a traditional Mother's Day mother lawn roll.

Go into the black ghetto of your town and call everyone you see a "mothah." A variation is to go up and ask them, "How's your mothah?" If you are black, go into a white ghetto. If you are Albanian, forget it.

Arbor Day

Keep telling people that Arbor Day spelled backward is Yad Robra, until this elicits a laugh.

Do not go to bed until you find someone who can explain to you the meaning of Arbor Day.

If you are Albanian forget both of these.

Father's Day

Go to department stores before Father's Day and try to find a decent-looking necktie.

On the day after Father's Day take all the ugly neckties anyone's ever given you and try to return them to a local store.

Invite everyone over for a traditional Father's Day father lawn roll.

Go into your local black ghetto and tell everyone there that you are a father and that they are a mothah. If you are black, do this in an Albanian neighborhood.

Independence Day

Go to a street one block away from where your community is having it's local Fourth of July parade. Stand on the corner by yourself and frantically wave a little American flag.

March in the Fourth of July parade dressed as a veteran of King Arthur's Wars.

Invite your friends over for the traditional Fourth of July firecracker lawn roll and firecracker hunt. Before everyone starts to roll and search, light the firecrackers.

Paint a room in your house red, white, and blue and put stars on the ceiling. Do not use a ladder. For extra toning, do not use a brush.

Try to make an American Legioneer of Foreign Wars laugh or smile while he is in the Fourth of July parade.

Labor Day

Do all the labor possible.

If possible, go into labor.

Hunt for Jimmy Hoffa.

Halloween

Paint your head orange.

Sit on your front porch with your mouth open and a lighted candle in your mouth.

Dress up as all the members of the New York Giants football team.

Try to have sex with a skeleton.

Dress up like Willie Nelson and try to get into a restaurant that has a dress code.

Clean out a pumpkin with your hands tied behind your back.

Dress up as Mayor Bradley of Los Angeles and do not go to sleep until someone recognizes who you are.

Go trick-or-treating by knocking on the windows of the second floor of each house you come to.

Disguise yourself as a hundred-year-old person. Spend several hours walking to the corner of your street.

Disguise yourself as the husband of a separated, feuding couple and try to get into the wife's apartment.

Buy an E.T. costume that is the exact size of E.T. and try to get into it.

Dress up as Quasimodo with an iron hump on your back.

Dress up as a New York bag lady and go trick-or-treating. Do not go home until you have a full bag of candy.

Election Day

Help the political party of your choice by walking through graveyards and picking out deceased voters' names for it.

Go to party headquarters and every few seconds toss your hat into the air, yelling, "Yippee, we're going to win!"

Veterans Day

Get into your old uniform and do a deep-knee bend. Sew up your pants.

Storm a beach.

Dress up as a Vietnam veteran and do not stop walking until somebody comes up to you and thanks you for the job you did over there.

Thanksgiving

Dress up as a turkey and join the other turkeys waiting to be slaughtered.

Dress up as a cooked turkey and place yourself in the center of your dining room table for your guests.

Clean out a pumpkin for pie with your hands tied behind your back, and forget that you did the same thing for Halloween.

Slice or carve the turkey with a spoon.

Invite a group of militant Indians over for Thanksgiving.

Dress as a turkey and go to a turkey shoot.

Have a big Thanksgiving dinner: turkey, stuffing, cranberries, sweet potatoes, pumpkin pie, the works. Do not use utensils.

After you eat Thanksgiving dinner, lean back, stretch, and yawn. Find all your buttons.

Buy a turkey and start stuffing it. Keep stuffing it. Don't stop.

Place each foot in a roasted turkey and take a nice long walk.

Buy a live turkey. Take it home, scream into its ear that you are going to chop off its head, and start chasing it.

Christmas

Decorate yourself as a Christmas Tree.

Dress up as Santa Claus and try to get down a chimney.

Take a sleigh ride through the park, but play the horse.

Go into a women's prison wearing mistletoe on your head.

Go into a men's prison wearing mistletoe on your head.

Go into a men's prison dressed like a woman, wearing a cluster of mistletoe on your head.

Take an old chair or other piece of furniture from your home and the day after Christmas try to return it to the local department store.

Visit the local department store's Santa Claus. Get in line and sit in his lap, dressed as a Hasidic Jew.

Dress as Santa Claus and try to sit in the lap of a Hasidic Jew.

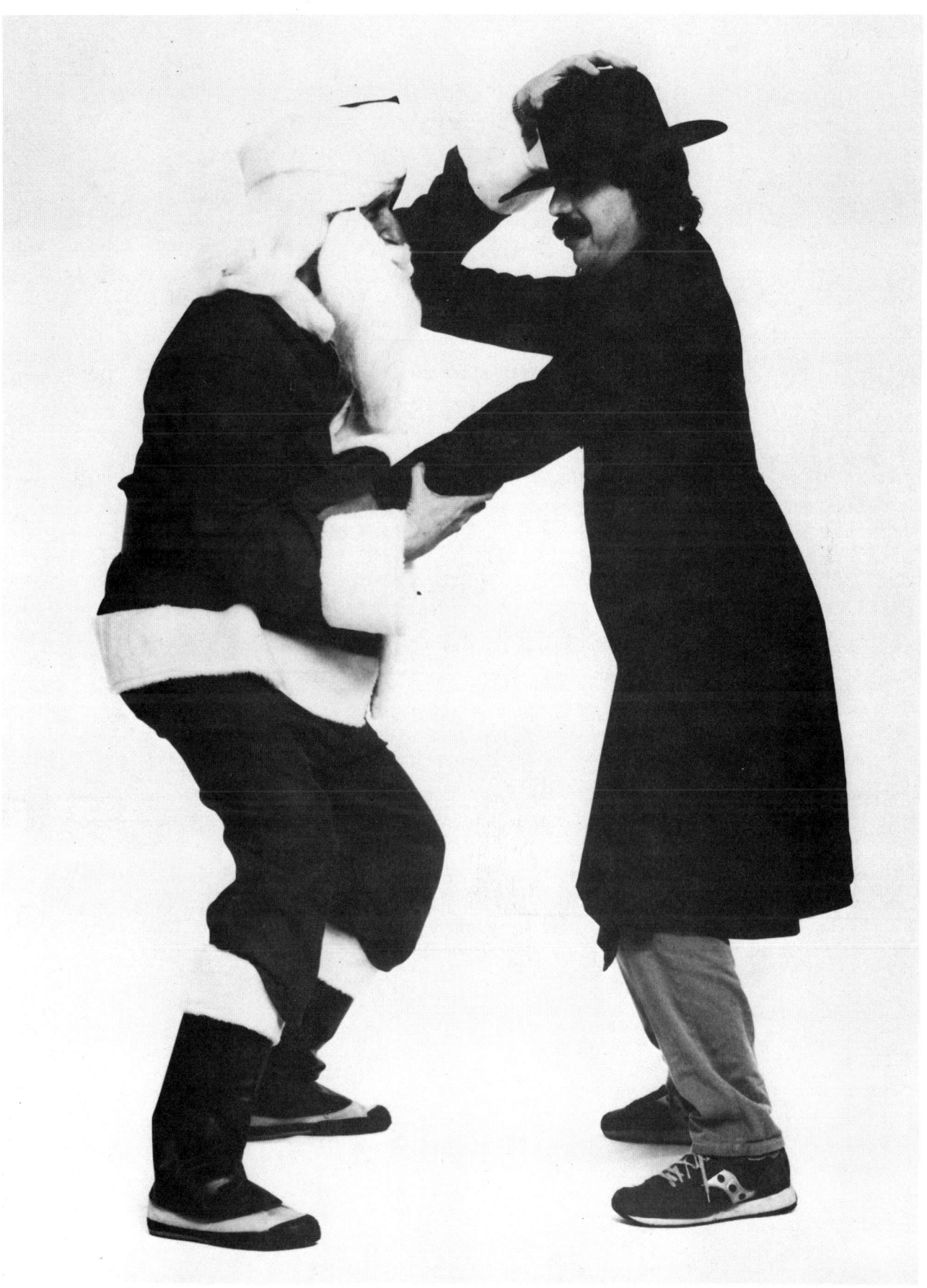

New Year's Eve

Go out and make an ass of yourself the way you do every New Year's Eve.

Go to a gay party dressed as a New Year's Eve baby.

Wherever you are, start the New Year's countdown four hours before midnight. Start at 14,400, 14,399, 14,398 . . .

Start running around celebrating New Year's on December 8.

Make Believe

A lot of weight can be lost and muscles toned by the exercise, actually the art form, of make believe. This is probably the highest form of art in the realm of exercise. I have listed some suggestions. Other areas can be created by you. Whatever you do, just remember: imagination doesn't cost anything and doesn't weigh anything. It can be your best friend. So now let us make believe you are . . .

A Traffic Patrol Officer
Stand in the middle of the busiest intersection in your town that is not controlled by a traffic policeman and direct traffic. For added excitement, dress up as a large chicken or Quasimodo. For even more excitement, wear a blindfold.

A Spy
This is a wonderful game to play, especially at night. You must always be on guard for opposing spies. Look over your shoulder constantly. Whip around corners and rush across crowded streets. Worry that some member of the opposition will have his .357 magnum, with a silencer, ready to wipe you out.

The Last Heterosexual
By imagining that you are the one human being who can satisfy the opposite sex you will find yourself constantly dodging them. These short leaps off the sidewalk and dashes across the street or up long flights of stairs will get you into unbelievable shape. A variation on this exercise is to make believe you are the only gay person in the world and that everyone knows it.

The Sole Survivor
Pretend everyone in the world has a communicable disease except for you. Then avoid people.

Jane Fonda
Make believe you are Jane Fonda. Wear leg warmers and count your money.

The New Yorker
Make believe you are living in New York. Run for cover every time you hear a car backfire.

Apartment Hunting
Make believe you need an apartment even if you don't and go apartment hunting.

Michael Jackson
Make believe you are winning a Grammy. Climb the stairs in your home at least eight or nine times. On the last climb remove your sunglasses. Then look for your other glove.

The Veterinarian
Make believe you are an animal doctor. Try to neuter as many German shepherds and Doberman pinschers as possible.

The Perfect Person
Make believe you are in absolutely perfect shape. Take this book and throw it into the nearest receptacle. Now realize who you really are and go in there and get it back, dammit.

A Parent
If you are not married or are married but have no children, buy an assortment of roller skates, balloons, crayons, balls, etc. and leave them all around your home. Scream as though you have children, stooping to pick up these items and putting them away in their proper places.

A Weatherman
On a clear day make believe you heard the weatherman predict torrential rainstorms. Wear a rubber raincoat and carry a heavy umbrella. On a springlike day act as if the weatherman had predicted a cold front and wear a heavy coat. If it gets too heavy, carry it.

Living in a Cold-Water Flat
Make believe you are living in a cold-water flat and that your superintendent does not provide enough heat. Get a stick, wooden hanger, or small hammer and pound on your radiator. If you don't have a radiator, buy an old used one and keep it in the house as though it were not working.

When You . . .
Do This

When You . . .	*Do This*
slap a mosquito	slap it twice.
run to catch a bus	run backward.
light a fireplace	use a steel log.
eat at a banquet	sit without a chair.
eat at a banquet	sit three feet from the table.
smoke	smoke an all-filter cigarette.
go to a symphony (not rock) concert	squirm to stay awake through the entire performance.
write postcards	use a quill pen.
eat a banana	don't peel it, squeeze it.
when a dentist puts his hand in your mouth	bite it.
water plants	use an eyedropper.
go to the beach	walk sideways like a crab.
go to a dinner party	fence with the little hors d'oeuvre swords.
yawn	keep your mouth closed.
yawn	give the Tarzan yell.
pick your teeth	use a comb.
rake leaves	use your hands.
read a book	act out all the verbs.
turn off the bed lamp	hold the light bulb and turn the lamp.
eat spaghetti	twirl the dish.
sit down	cross your leg over someone else's leg, preferably a stranger.
sit down	cross your right leg over your left and keep it that way, even when you get up to walk away.
wear slacks	leave your belt at home.
put stamps on an envelope	use dry stamps.
give your seat to a lady	take one from a man.
tip your hat	hold your hat and lower your head.
dry yourself off after a shower	use a washcloth.
undress at night	remove your undergarmets first.

When You . . .	*Do This*
pass a suspicious-looking person	scream.
ride in a taxi	check the meter every ten seconds.
applaud	hold both hands behind your back.
fly a prop/commuter plane	carry your own parachute.
look through the Yellow Pages	look through every single page, and use different fingers to walk or jog through it.

NOTE: When you use the little finger and the ring finger, you will walk through the Yellow Pages with a limp, but don't let that bother you.

walk to work	wear a kosher pickle in your underwear.

NOTE: Remember that giggling tones you up.

bob for apples at a party	try the local river or lake, or your whirlpool, Jacuzzi, or dishwasher.
go to confession	press your face as hard as you can against the wire mesh.
watch TV that is captioned for the hard of hearing	imitate the lady in the corner of the screen.
see a group of Hare Krishnas	walk up and yell, "What does a guy have to do to get flowers around here?"
walk down the street	hail every cab you see.
travel in a foreign country	wear a U.S. Marine colonel's uniform.
finger paint	use only your face.

NOTE: For even greater results try using the face of an Italian.

park your car under a tree	sit on the hood and try to avoid bird droppings.
rewind your cassette tapes	do it manually.
pass a construction site	find a tough-looking construction worker who is above the eighth floor. Act like the foreman and wave frantically for him to come down for a conversation with you. Leave before he gets there.

When You . . .	*Do This*
when your dog goes into heat	take her for a walk.
stomp out a cigarette	twist both feet, swinging your hands; occasionally jump in the air.
wait in a bank line	jump rope with the divider.
go through a revolving door	make ten revolutions.
swim and have to go to the bathroom	get out of the water and go.
hang a hammock	hang it high enough so you have to jump into it.
wait at the airport for your luggage	walk on the conveyor belt to find your bags.
play with the loose change in your pockets	don't use your hands.
play cards	use fewer people so you can shuffle more.

Thinking to Burn Up Fat

It is a little-known fact, but nevertheless scientifically true, that thinking consumes a lot of energy. It burns up calories almost as quickly as physical exercise. The harder you think, the more energy you use. So give yourself a real tough problem to think about—something to ponder. The following are suggestions of what to think about.

The names of twenty-five famous Italian war heroes

Ten Spanish songs that do not contain the word corazón

The reason why Rubik's Cube was so popular

Twenty-five substantial reasons why you should get married or stay married

One substantial reason why you should get married or stay married

Ten vital lessons that you learned in your twelve years at school

Five honest politicians

Twenty reasons you should move to Cincinnati

Twenty-five countries that are not at war or in a revolution

If the three blind mice couldn't see, how could they run after the farmer's wife? More important, if they could see, would they have run after the farmer's wife?

Why Michael Jackson wears only one glove

How many more shopping days there are until Christmas

What's so great about Alan Alda

Why you spent so much money on this book

Why David Brenner wrote this book

What David Brenner is going to do with all the money you just gave him for this book

Miscellaneous Helpful Hints

Try to give the "high five" slap to only very tall people.

Shoot craps with round dice.

Stand in an unemployment line once a week, even if you have a job. Shift your weight from one leg to the other. Get angry.

Go to a maternity ward and pace up and down as though your wife were in labor. If you make believe it is a girl friend, you will lose more weight and burn off more calories. If you make believe she is of a different race and your mother is coming over any minute, you will really tighten up.

Go into a Polish neighborhood on a Friday night and walk across the lanes of the local bowling alley.

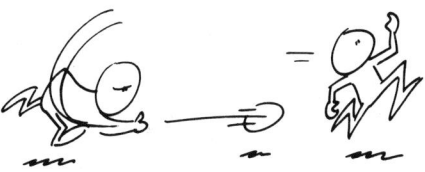

Put a bocce ball in each pocket of your clothing.

Visit your proctologist daily for one year.

Attach a store mannequin to you and play Siamese twins for a day.

Try to work a digital watch without using your hands.

Go through an entire day wearing someone else's glasses.

Have a daily supply of Mexican water sent to your home.

When running for a bus, drop your pants around your ankles.

When you get up in the morning, lie flat on your back on the floor, legs together, arms by your side. Now stay there. Tomorrow is another day.

Chase the L.A. Raiders and yell, "Alzado sucks!"

Make believe you lost a contact lens and help the good samaritans who have offered to help you look for it.

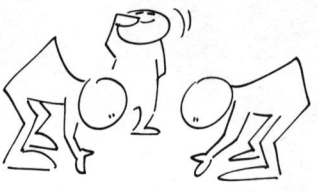

Try to forget the Alamo.

Every cloud has a silver lining. Try to find one.

There are fifty ways to leave your lover. Try to get away with just one of them.

Track down your old high school bully. Call him up and give him your name and address and tell him you still think he sucks.

When you go on a vacation, take your spouse with you. The tension will just explode away your fat and tighten the muscles throughout your entire body.

It is a scientific fact that people burn up more calories and use more energy when they are in a state of panic. Therefore, whenever you have the opportunity, even the slightest provocation, go into a trauma. For example, a sugar donut is delivered to the office instead of a plain donut. Panic. Pace. Throw up your arms. Have a fit. Panic some more.

Offer to carry a teenager's ghetto blaster.

Stretching is very important. As often as possible make change with your feet.

Buy a trumpet and practice by blowing in the wrong end.

Stand alongside or behind two black men and pretend you're one of the Pips. Or with two friends (preferably white or Chinese) stand behind a black woman and make believe you are a Pip. If you are a man, dress as a woman; if you are a woman, just stand in front of three black men and make believe you're Gladys Knight.

Try to open bottles with child-proof caps. Once this is accomplished, put the cap back on and repeat the process.

Jumping is good for you. Play checkers.

Buy a copy of War and Peace and use it as a fly swatter.

Grab a complete stranger and try to act out the cover of a paperback romance.

Read William F. Buckley's latest book, moving your head between it and the dictionary.

To build up your neck muscles go to a library or book store and try to read the book titles on the spines. Do not cheat by turning them so they read horizontally.

Calorie-Burning Activities

The following is a list of activities and the number of calories they burn. Never before divulged in any exercise book or pamphlet, these facts have been completely researched, tested, validated, and confirmed. Everything you are about to read is gospel.

Activity	*Calories* (burned per minute)
Staring straight ahead	50
Staring upward	55
Staring downward	55
Blinking one eye at a time	60
Blinking both eyes at the same time	75
Smacking lips after a meal	30
Smacking lips for no reason	40
Smacking someone else's lips	50
Speaking pig Latin	25
Speaking pig Latin backward	40
Speaking pig Latin to a Latin	45
Speaking pig Latin to a pig	50
Speaking pig Latin to a Latin pig	60
Listening to a pig speaking Latin	75
Remembering the capital of Wyoming	20
Wearing a moose costume for Halloween	65
Wearing no costume for Halloween	75
Wearing a moose costume other than on Halloween	80
Wearing a *real* moose either on Halloween or any other time	120
Hunting moose	80
Fishing for moose	160
Crossing the Delaware River in a boat	30
Swimming the Delaware River	45
Swimming the Delaware River inside of a boat	105
Crossing yourself while on a riverboat	50
Asking directions to Kutztown, PA	20
Giving directions to Kutztown, PA	25
Living in Kutztown, PA	110

Activity	Calories (burned per minute)
Wearing loafers	20
Wearing loafers while sitting	30
Wearing loafers while running	40
Wearing loafers while watching a Humphrey Bogart movie	50
Wearing loafers while loafing	5
Wearing loafers while eating a loaf of bread	10
Wearing a loaf of bread while eating loafers	60
Trying to remember these loafer jokes	90
Drawing a sardine	40
Drawing Sardinia	50
Drawing a Sardinian sardine	75
Counting to 98	40
Counting to 98.6	45
Retrieving one's underwear from a bulldog	140
Retrieving one's underwear from a Doberman pinscher	160
Retrieving a Doberman pinscher's underwear	180
Trying to put it on	200
Putting your underwear on a Doberman pinscher and then trying to retrieve it	400
Pronouncing properly all United Nations countries	60
Pronouncing all United Nations countries backward	70
Pronouncing the names of all the backward United Nations countries	75
Putting extra stamps on an envelope	80
Successfully tossing a tissue into the wastebasket	30
Operating a piece of heavy machinery while on antihistamines	50
Marching to Washington for a worthy cause	100
Marching to Washington for a lousy cause	120
Marching to Washington for no cause	140
Wondering what Michael Jackson is doing at this very moment	30
Wondering what Jesse Jackson is doing at this very moment	35
Wondering what Jesse James is doing at this very moment	50
Wondering what Rick James is doing at this very moment	55
Wondering about blacks	65
Humming the song "Is You Is or Is You Ain't My Baby"	80
Wondering if John Denver looks Jewish	40
Wondering if John Denver ever looked at anyone who is Jewish	50
Wondering if Toulouse Lautrec really knew he was short	50
Scratching yourself above the belt	50
Scratching yourself below the belt	60
Scratching someone else above or below the belt	100
Opening a window	30
Opening a window with a chair	50

Activity	*Calories* (burned per minute)
Opening a window with a ham	60
Breakdancing	100
Breaking something while you are dancing	250
Running to turn off the radio when you hear "You Light Up My Life"	100
Running to turn off the radio when you hear "My Way"	200
Nursing a hangover	80
Nursing someone with a hangover	90
Hanging over a nurse	100
Nursing a nurse	100
Jumping for joy	60
Jumping *with* joy	70
Jumping *on* Joy	120
Enjoying jumping on Joy	140
Beating around the bush	30
Beating a bush	40
Singing "Trouble Right Here in River City"	40
Acting out "Trouble Right Here in River City"	140
Understanding the AT&T breakup	160
Swallowing your pride	120
Swallowing someone else's pride	140
Waiting for a 7-11 to close	80
Twiddling your thumbs	20
Thumbing your twiddles	120
Avoiding an issue	30
Issuing an avoidance	40
Jumping to a conclusion	80
Jumping the gun	90
Running rampant	100
Shredding paper	40
Shredding paper without a paper shredder	60
Making something out of nothing	75
Jumping on the bandwagon	85
Jumping on the bandwagon while it's moving	110
Pondering if it's Ella or Memorex	40
Trying to teach an old dog new tricks	50
Trying to get an old trick to go with a new dog	85
Pounding a nail	30
Getting nailed	40
Getting nailed in bed	140
Getting nailed on a bed of nails	160
Controlling your own destiny	40
Holding back a sneeze	100

Activity	Calories (burned per minute)
Sneezing on someone's back	125
Holding back when someone sneezes on your back	150
Making it on a water bed	30
Making it *in* a water bed	50
Making it with a water bed	100
Throwing something	40
Throwing something down	50
Throwing something up	60
Making a mountain out of a molehill	140
Making out with a mole on a mountain	340
Trying to get a new roll of toilet paper started	95
Brushing your teeth	30
Brushing your hair	40
Brushing your teeth with your hair	60
Brushing someone else's hair and/or teeth	80
Leaving in a huff	90
Going with the flow	95
Getting the inside scoop	60
Shaking your leg	40
Shaking someone else's leg	50
Shaking a leg of lamb	60
Shaking a lamb	70
Watching a *G*-rated movie	40
Watching an *X*-rated moves	80
Starring in an *X*-rated movie	120
Starring in an *X*-rated movie with a lamb	140
Starring in an *X*-rated movie with a leg of lamb	160
Counting the humps on a camel	90
Counting on humping a camel	100
Smoking a Camel after humping one	200

Sports

No exercise book would be complete without addressing the area of sports. Americans, probably more than any other people in the world, are sports oriented. We'll play, watch, read, or talk about anything that involves any kind of inflated sphere, or anything that can be thrown, kicked, or hit to a base, through a basket, or for a goal. If you were to blow up a squirrel's ass and start to bounce it down the street, you could have a team within ten minutes. We love sports. I, too, love sports and am the last person to knock them; I realize, like everyone else, that sports activity is important. However, one can overdo it.

I have always had the philosophy that once you reach the age of twenty-one you have to stop playing with a ball. Another way to look at it is, once you reach an annual income of $10,000, you should be careful crossing the street. This also means you should stop playing with a ball. I know, however, that all of you want to continue playing your sports, and I would not discourage you. Here are extra ways of losing weight and toning up while enjoying your favorite personal sport activities.

Bowling
When bowling, ignore the buzzer when you cross the foul line and run all the way down to the pins before releasing the ball.

Don't put your fingers in the holes of the ball.

Tennis
Play tennis without a racket.
Play tennis with a baseball bat.
Watch a fast-moving tennis match, using only your eyes.
Play tennis using a Barbie-doll racquet.

Biking
Buy an exercise bike and carry it to a different room every day.

Frisbee
Throw a Frisbee and the next day go look for it.

Walking
Leave your shoes at home and go to the beach on a hot July day when the sun is glaring. Try to take a casual stroll on the sand.

Weightlifting
Do exactly that, only change it from weight to wait. Wait. You have a lot of time to strain yourself.

Basketball
Play basketball with a deflated ball and do a lot of dribbling.

Think of all the people with whom you'd like to get even. Feel the adrenaline shoot through your body, tighten up those muscles from cheeks to shins, get your blood boiling. Now go after them! Revenge is the best exercise!

Conclusion

I hope that what you have read is going to be an enormous help to your physical, mental, and eventually your social well-being. I am a firm believer in staying in shape without causing oneself pain or aggravation. I truly believe that if you were to follow every suggestion in this book, within, let's say, six months you would be transformed into a total schmuck.

However, I do want to leave you on a positive note. How does B-flat strike you? No? I would like to take the time right here to tell you of one honest-to-goodness, serious, easy-to-do, totally beneficial exercise. The truth of the matter is that I have a chronic back problem, and I am limited in my ability to exercise. The following is an exercise that was suggested to me by one of my favorite human beings, Dr. Milton Reder of New York City. It works, honestly. It's fun, honestly. You'll love doing it, honestly. You'll feel like an idiot while you're doing it, honestly. The exercise consists of going into a body of water—a pool, lake, or ocean—up to your chin and jogging for twenty minutes, taking a ten-minute break, and then going back in and jogging for another twenty minutes. The water keeps you buoyant and prevents you from straining any of your joints, such as ankles or knees, or damaging your internal organs, and the resistance of the water acts as a toning device. It is perfectly safe and will keep you in shape. The only precaution is to be sure that the water level never goes above your forehead. Once you get between one and six feet under water, jogging becomes more difficult, as does breathing. It is recommended that you do not wear street clothes during this exercise. I would also suggest that you do not do this exercise in the shipping lanes.

Keep in mind that it was the great Greek athlete Aristotle Coliditus—considered to this day to be one of the finest physical specimens of all time—who said in Athens, in the company of Plato and Socrates, "Exercise, who needs it? Pass me a gyro sandwich. I hate to go to an orgy on an empty stomach."

THE END

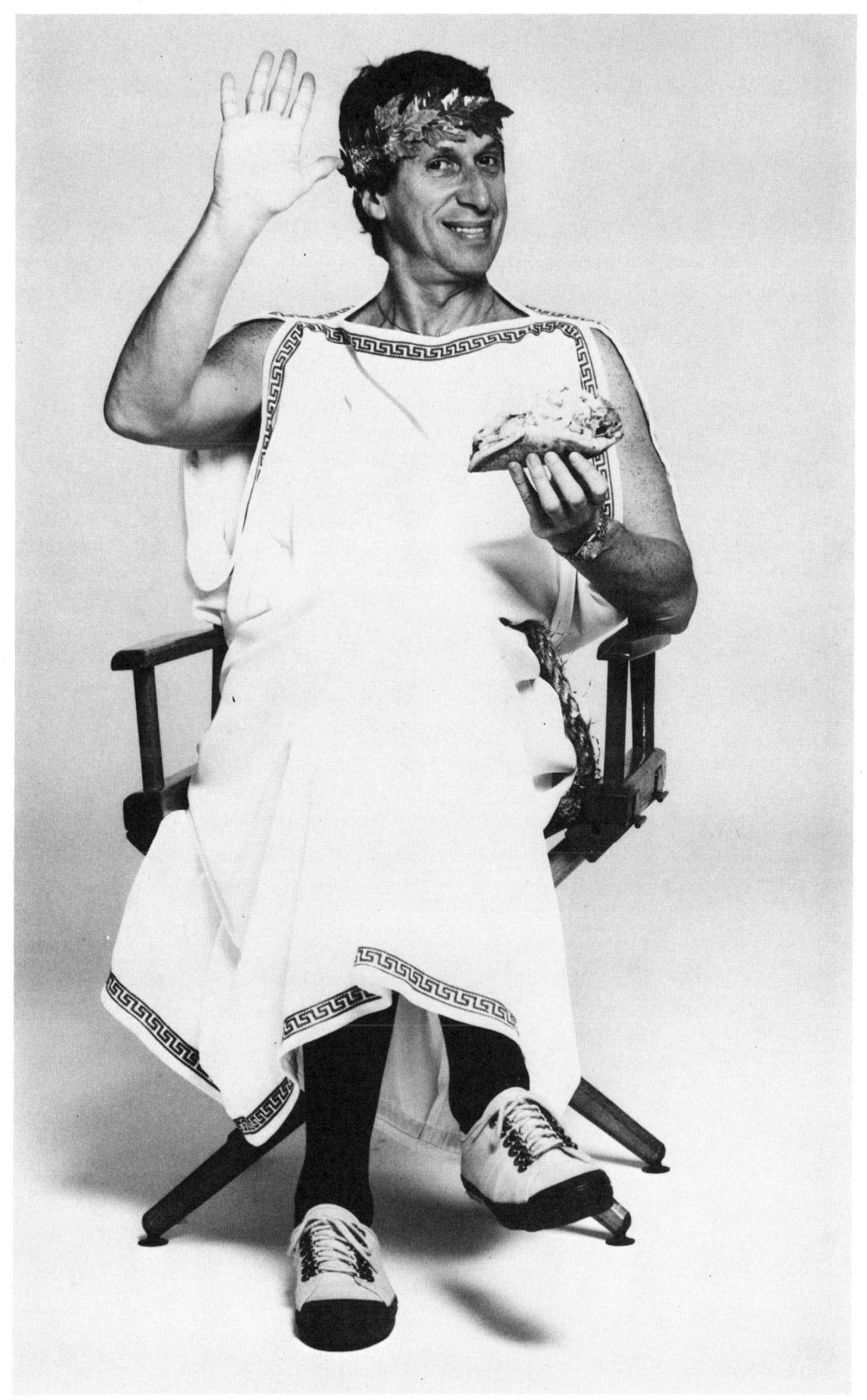